THE NOWHERE BIRDS

Caitríona O'Reilly

THE NOWHERE BIRDS

BLOODAXE BOOKS

ISBN: 1 85224 560 3

First published 2001 by
Bloodaxe Books Ltd,
Highgreen,
Tarset,
Northumberland NE48 1RP.

Bloodaxe Books Ltd acknowledges
the financial assistance of Northern Arts.

Cover printing by J. Thomson Colour Printers Ltd, Glasgow.

Printed in Great Britain by
Cromwell Press Ltd, Trowbridge, Wiltshire.

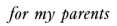

for my parents

Acknowledgements

Acknowledgements are due to the editors of the following publications in which some of these poems first appeared: *Books Ireland, Brangle, College Green, Heat* (Sydney), *The Irish Times, Metre, New Writing* (Picador/British Council, 2001), *Nua* (Tennessee), *Oxford Poetry, Poetry Ireland Review, Stream and Gliding Sun* (Wicklow, 1998), *Thumbscrew* and *Verse*.

A number of these poems were broadcast on the Cúrsaí Ealaíne programme on RTE television, and on Lyric FM. Others featured in the 4 + 4 @ 4 exhibition of Women Poets and Artists of the South-East in 1999.

I am also grateful to The Arts Council/An Chomhairle Ealaíon for a generous grant in 1999.

Contents

The bland and sculped and urgent beasts,
The here and there and nowhere birds,
The tongues of fire, the words of foam,
The curdling stars in the night's dome –
This is on me and these are yours.

LOUIS MACNEICE
'A Toast'

Perdita

I cannot feel found.
I filled your absence in me
with all the wrong things, father,
fardels, odd bits, gewgaws,
waves in tendrils and trees like lobster claws
and howling. Being chased.
There's a mesh of dark inside my head
behind the face
purely my mother's –
like air shelled in light, a purple bubble,
the thin skin over a scream.

Fragment

This night-breathing deceives, it is so calm.
The headland glitters with beached faces, lunar stares,
a tidal moon-haul of wrecks and drownings.
Their gazes are blank and lasting,
outfacing constellations even, crystalline.

My mother feared the wash and plunge,
that huge pull from the loosening shore.
Night after night she surfaced there again
in the small hours, the shallows, panting:
her near death refreshed by nightmare.

A child, I shut my eyes like oysters
on the green light, weird particles migrating upwards
from the bed, from whose choked throat
arose the swallow-sound I'd closed my ears on.
Now as I watch her sleeping and submerged

I see them, those obsessive dead –
their watery features sea-blurred, merged, evasive.
I hold my breath above her sinking head,
dreading their opaque past and fossil histories,
inky and indistinct as night water.

Six

The blond medallions of the aspen
shook and burned on the first day

of summer. I wore my gingham pinny
and no knickers and waved wildly

at the boats rounding the bay,
snagging the waters to a silver V.

Granny had her wound dressed
as usual in her cool dark room.

Mummy made scrambled eggs for tea.
Charlie and I jumped like fleas

off the old stone house and fell
giggling to the grassy bank.

One, two, three steps back
for a good long run, four, five, six...

I stepped into nothing.
Fragments of green and brown glass

tore the gingham pinafore
as I came to and Charlie stared

frog-eyed at my arm, bent
improbably back at the elbow.

In hospital, Kermit looked peeved
about the confiscated chocolates

and sulked at the end of my bed.
Granny saw gingham in her dreams,

vanishing over a cliff-edge.
Every day the student doctors came

and took more notes, staring
and rattling their stethoscopes.

I fretted in the wicker chair,
inserting a knitting-needle

inside the dusty cast, always
missing the itch by inches.

I couldn't tell what I'd broken.
Charlie was suddenly childish,

and anyway, he was a boy.
I collected autographs and pouted.

When they finally sawed the cast off,
my arm, like a helium balloon, floated.

Ninety Eighty-Four

Saint Laurence O'Toole meant business
with his high cheekbones and stiff mitre.
Mary wore lipstick and no shoes
so I sat on her side of the altar.

She wasn't frightening at all
as with her halo at a rakish angle,
she trod on plaster clouds and stars
behind a row of five pence candles.

She always appeared ignorant
of her swelling middle, or
even politely averted her eyes
(and she never got any bigger).

Later on I couldn't look
for fear she might suddenly move.
That year whole crowds of Marys
wept bloody tears in their groves,

making signs with fragmented hands.
And I knew or guessed why –
the worst thing a schoolgirl could do
was to give birth alone and die

under Mary's hapless supervision.
No apparitions in grottoes
or wingèd babies with cradle-cap
for the likes of those.

Diary of a Conformist

It always seems the clouds move
with restless ceremonial from the West
and the small birds shriek and toss
their bodies to the wind like empty gloves.
I wonder whether seagulls cry or laugh
and pray I might be one of them at last

if it means escape from the top bunk bed
and the cracks in the ceiling, the swollen tonsils,
the doll's house and colouring pencils.
Where the gable bisects the potting shed
is a blue triangle the size of my head
over which gulls sometimes pass, their tensile

cries like steel wire, their guts unravelling
grotesquely down the garden in the end,
victims of the tabby-cat and wind,
mincemeat made of their wings' corbelling.
Heaven knows what the thermometer's telling
my mother, as she waves it around like a wand.

Later, when she switches off the light
the willow-patterned wallpaper grows ears
and eyes and tusks and trunks, while near
the door are dogs with eyes like dinner-plates.
Outside, Stephen's open-mouthed granny sits
digesting wicked children as they pass her.

I am certain I have woken up
since the sky this morning is the colour
of washed gold, as when storm-clouds blow over.
I unknot my hair and do my school tie up
and swallow my porridge. On the front step
I turn to examine the face of my mother.

She nods blankly as ever. I catch my breath.
Surely she's noticed that something's amiss?
All along the road the tarmac hisses
and bubbles up and spits like witches' broth
and gives off such a stench it's hard to breathe,
while the trees suppurate as if rinsed

in acid, frothing and barkless and bare.
The walk to school is like a dream
I've had before of a forgotten scene
where the leaves on the bushes writhe and roar
and the sky reddens. Except that here
the light is gentle and the sky is clean.

And in school they teach me to remember,
remember my nine-times table. Father Geoghegan
tells us the story of the wise and foolish virgins:
*Watch therefore, for ye know not the day nor
the hour...* But isn't the day already over?
Or is it just that night and day are merging?

I've decided that after all I haven't woken,
because all the clouds are coming from the East
today, although the wind is in the West.
And the sun still shines and no bones are broken
and in the bay the yachts are taken
in the swing of the swell, their masts

ticking and ticking like metronomes.
I believe in the faces of my father and mother.
Their smiles are my prevailing weather.
I believe in the sanctity of the home.
I believe in the detail in the carpet and the see of Rome.
The family that prays together stays together.

Two Night Time Pieces

Pisces

Thirteen Februaries slept through
before I learned what going under meant.

Pale and thin as sheets,
the near fields burst free of mooring.

Then the turn of the tide,
the sea stack,

the pier-light's onyx eye.
Those teenage dreams

were cuttle-ink tattoos
describing blue-rinse mermen,

each muscular wave awash
with sex and phosphor.

I was awash and rocked,
rocked hard to wake

and woke, drenched to the roots,
my flannelette pyjamas stiff with sand.

Sleep and Spiders

It is too strange to kill.
The symmetry of its eyes,

its eight paired legs askew
on the lintel, exoskeletal

and tiger-striped, all digestion.
It looks sudden but is still

for hours, eyes on stalks,
awaiting news from hair-triggers

that might be legs or fingers
(the whole thing a claw)

come to touch me in sleep –
hammock from which

black shadows seep.
Stars go milky, then go out.

I wake at five to what five is –
a cold blue glow and a self

trussed, barely breathing,
paralytic with dreams.

Thin

It is chill and dark in my small room.
A wind blows through gaps in the roof,
piercing even the eiderdown. My skin
goose-pimples in front of the cloudy glass
though there was scalding tea for dinner
with an apple. I'm cold to the bone.

I don't sleep well either. My hip-bones
stick in the foam mattress, and the room's
so empty. My sister is having dinner
with a boy. Awake under the roof
I watch the stars bloom heavily through glass
and think, *how shatterproof is my skin?*

I doze till six, then drink semi-skim
milk for breakfast (the bare bones
of a meal) before nine o'clock class.
It's kind of hard to leave my room
for the walk to school. No roof
over me, and eight solid hours till dinner-

time. All day my dreams of dinner
are what really get under my skin,
not the boys. My tongue sticks to the roof
of my mouth again in class. I'm such a bone-
head! And my stomach's an empty room.
My face floats upwards in a glass

of Coke at lunchtime. One glass.
I make it last the whole day till dinner:
hot tea and an apple in my room.
My sister seems not to notice the skin
around my mouth or my ankle-bones.
If our parents knew they'd hit the roof

I suppose. My ribs rise like the roof
of a house that's fashioned from glass.
I might even ping delicately like bone-
china when flicked. No dinner
for six weeks has made this skin
more habitable, more like a room –

or a ceiling that shatters like glass
over those diners off gristle and bone.
This skin is a more distinguished room.

Envy

This was your dream, an illusion of perpetual departure
from darkened doorways, crackling upper floors
whose light your eyes absorbed like stolen silver.
And a crooked sign hung where the sun was
in the dull sky, dangerous as radium.
There was an ink-blot or bluish burn on your thigh
that meant exposure. You went on dreaming nevertheless,
down the thin streets with their high walls,
courtyards filled with bodies of stone, cypresses,
and the linden tree, prodigal within limits.
You woke with fingermarks around your bony wrists.

Pandora's Box

I might lift the eaves again
and startle a small room still lit from within
and finger the traces I left there.

The considerations of days
lurk behind porous walls.
They cling there like stains.

Carpets soaked in the seepage of dreams,
flakes of skin
piled on surfaces as thick as dust.

There's a head-shape in the pillow
like a big fingerprint.
Memories flutter up like insects –

small shrieks, minor crimes inside
an inked-up window-pane
with clotted stars,

and now, outside the shut box,
this black beach with an ocean on it
breathing in waves,

tiered like plate glass,
and the whole world at night-time
a wide sea full of starfish waiting to be caught.

Proserpine

When the light from the narrow window falls on their last
        quiet meeting and this man's face is frozen
she remembers his eyes like two drowsy animals and his mouth
        and the back of his head like a boy's head, a ripened apple.

She remembers this in the light from the narrow window
        as he turns away into darkness and the smell of the soil.
His sleep is hard as a stone and what his smile says
        only the statues know in their halved limbs, their bones.

While her secret ripens far underground she tries and she tries
        with this boy to burst the stained heart of the fruit
and spreads her green skirt wide under the clouds the rain the sun
        the parched stars of the sky in August

but the man who was turned to stone sheds himself
        inside her dream like light from narrow windows she remembers
his eyes two quiet animals his head ripe as an apple
        as a boy's head as she wakes with a throatful of loam

The Red Man

For how many nights now
has he waited, angry and hungry?
He'll never be filled, the red man
whose object is to puncture skin
and swallow the débris of decades.
Brickbats, shells and hypodermics
nestle with the tideline's other ordure
there inside the red man's skull.
He follows me into shockproof
steel and concrete buildings
till in a cold corridor we meet,
or waits in a tunnel of himself
to tear his hair and fulminate
and call me all the cunts under the sun.
And when he cuts he expects me to grin,
the red man, who'll steal what's left
of the sky's colour for his own eyes
though he's a red man otherwise.

Autobiography

Here the weather has its own spectrum,
a seemingly limitless palette. To the north
a chain of swollen, dark green mountains.
Mostly they are smooth and stippled with heather,
then too I've seen them snow-capped, gleaming.
The run of mountains ends with the seaward
drop of Bray Head's ponderous mossy forehead.
Between there and here are miles of salty fields.
Clattering by on the littoral track after a flood
I've seen the miserable cattle islanded
on the high ground of their uneven fields.
In summer those meadows burn with gorse.
An intermittent shot to scare the birds
is all that disturbs the gelatinous air –
that, and the odd vertical string of bonfire smoke.
The distant hill on which my town is built quivers.
I live between three Victorian piers on the bay's industrial side.
The bay smiles, it is full of flattened shiny water
sucking quietly at the shore and piers. All night
I adjust my own breath to its eternally regular breaking.
Less frequently now, a cargo ship sets up
a prehistoric rumble in the waters of the bay
and docks, raising its hatches with a metal groan.
Two synchronised forklift trucks neatly stack
the planks of timber, balletic and mechanical.
When the ships brought raw cement, plumes of dust
would sweep across the bay, coating our windows and doors.
On the east side of my house is an ancient castle keep
of blackest rock, that leans like a fin
from the back of the sea. I live in the shadow
of the shadow of a castle's walls.
They have fallen to hummocks of bright grass
that we played in as children,
wriggling into nests and hidey-holes.
The dark beach in the lee of the castle
is where Saint Patrick put ashore. He soon left,
shocked at the natives' epic unfriendliness:
They knocked Saint Manntan's front teeth down his neck.

Among the shells and shingle of the beach
are opalescent nuggets of glass, rounded and stone-smooth
from aeons rolling on the ocean floor.
Was it really from wrecked galleons they came?
But still there is the bay's omega, its theatre of weather,
a glass bowl for the sky to play in. The sea has no colour
save what weather brings. I've watched the sky and sea
go up in flames at dusk, though mostly they're an angry grey.
Now any horizon of mine must be nine-tenths sky.

The Harbour in January

Maybe this landscape never frowned
and spoiled its early blue face.
Above, like an arched eyebrow,

a single crow makes broken circles.
Birds in the hedge confer in boiling voices.
It takes a large design to displace

mercury-heavy rolls like these –
water relaxing its folds of fabric.
It sees us bend from cockpit or quayside

and gives us shivering bodies, splintered
faces and hands. We aren't ourselves in it.
Like a glamorous uncrossed desert,

the sea's of mobile feature. Any ship's legacy
is a smile that widens and complicates
and gapes to take in all the bay and me –

not of the sea, not in it, just looking on
at how the purple undertow reveals itself
in surfacing, in lapsing platinum.

Blueness

The dark sky of Switzerland
was the edge of the sky. Black metal from heaven
shed heavy radiance there and the air burned blue.
Glaciers glittered in the distance, inching south.
    There was blue in the mountain's throat.

After a six week thaw
foamy snow survived in the valley's angles.
The sun dropped from sight early and steeply.
In its electric shadow, blue-white storms
    scoured the tops of the hills.

And all things at first were blue.
It soaks the heart, fills the papery skin
of infants with vascular colour. This purplish hue
shadowing the hollow of my ribs tells again
    how cold and blue I am.

Interlude

With its *gelati* and bougainvillea-draped sculpture,
Italy hovered like a rumour five miles further.
Binn was worthy, litterless, Swiss;

where to breathe was like a sea-plunge, even in June.
Populated by six-foot clean-limbed blondes,
they bled pure gold, if they bled at all. Anaemic Knut

('like *Hamsun*') was an exception. He composed
electronically ('like *Kraftwerk*') and afterwards
dropped by for *Kräutertee*. I'd never even heard of *Hunger*.

Hector, who had a scar from nipple to navel, called me 'pure'
in nasty English. There was a failed seduction
by a man with a handlebar moustache and gold tooth,

a silly crush on a stout-legged father of five...
The summer dragged to an end. Where the sun once fell
tremendously there was the noise of thunder.

I cracked the ice on the *bier-garten* tables, folded umbrellas,
bid a tender farewell to the urinals. A thousand pounds
in the heel of my shoe might have bought three months

in a Berlin flat. But in the airport a kitten wailed in a basket
dementedly and a jittery pilot sweated over his charts
and I was back, convincing them I'd ever been elsewhere.

Transition

In the dull pre-dawn dark
I wake to reports from the stricken zone.
The earth has torn itself like tissue overnight,
          the walls have fallen in.
I don't feel as ineffaceable as stone –
blond stones of Paris, the veined city,
Napoleon in porphyry at the heart of it.
          No casualty.
Shocked, I remove all trace of myself
from somewhere not my own, the lent flat.
...as long as the mirrors are quiet,
          the chrome left gleaming...
I extract the city from myself as easily.
The numb streets fade as I walk through them.
I'm already absent on the Métro
          in the thickening dawn
with the couple kissing on the opposite seat,
the airport stop, the terminal.
All I can see is the list
          of what my eyes will lose.
The dead wait under architraves for days.
What gets detained in stone is history.
And for once I'm glad to leave the ground
          despite my fear of heights,
my need for permanence. I swallow my tea.
*This turbulence we're now experiencing
was forecast*, says the captain, smoothly.

They Do It With Mirrors

She could have sworn the door was double locked
or what was that inside keyhole for?

He left in the morning, turning his key
against burglars and junkies, while she

drooled on the pillow of their broken bed
dry-socketed, after a botched extraction.

The occupants of a hundred jigsawed homes
silted the city's arteries. He was another one.

She slowly rose. The dim, mirrored room
had cracked wainscoting, which let the wind

but not the light in. It was not their flat.
Over coffee, the locked door stared her down

till she could have snapped the key in its slot.
Never broken into, the toughened steel grille

on the window loomed as she recalled
the unreachable wail of a walled-up child

while smoke dribbled from a crack in the brick.
It was not their flat. Was nothing to be forced?

The windows opposite might well have caught
her white divided face as she proved herself just

narrow enough to step clear, as from her own bones.
He'd wonder where she was when he got home.

Sunday

The Liffey twists inside its stone confines,
heedless. It has long since abjured protest,

saving images of nothing
but the rains and whimsy of a city sky.

It gains a wider heaven at the bay perhaps,
but at its own expense.

We walk among the parts of a stopped world
in the meantime, hearing it go by.

The noise of tearing metal
in the quayside wrecker's yard has ceased,

just the one car, wind-rocked and upended,
groaning slowly. Its wheels still spin.

As though we'd stumbled on catastrophe
without a clue to where the iron giants went

that lived here once. They left
an architecture vacant-faced and angular,

with windows smashed or empty,
refusing reflection. Our contact seems

transgressive here, and our joined hands falter
nearing that squat god menacing skywards:

an abandoned crane, dangling its black clamp
like a pendulum halted over our heads.

Statuary

I *The Crouching Boy*

They hold such broken attitudes
that once were strong enough to hold
their own in gleaming city-states –
now the marble flows in them
like burst mercury, making them fragments
of a dance to ring the room:
damaged patriarchs and footloose caryatids.

Only a waist-high boy, the centrepiece,
gives nothing of himself away.
His shoulders, knees, and uncreated hands
compose a vessel of shadows, from which
he'll grow to be himself again
and so endure, if never quite become:
stone boy contemplating stone.

II *Tall Figure in Studio*

I think I am as he wanted me –
the one upright amidst this studied dereliction,
the cobwebs choking on plaster-dust,
old splintered frames, stained mattresses and rubble.
I stand rigid, obsessed by my wire core
and the little else I am given,
this spoon-shaped pelvis, a suggestion of breasts –
in form an expression of all his withdrawals
through the days of my making,
or like a plucked string, remembering his fingers
as his final silence became proper sound.

III *Bargello*

When the air grew thick in the afternoons
we took to abandoned palaces.
Did we imagine that unreal angle of the floor
or did Giambologna's bronze birds
shift on their plinths?
There was a rumpus in the basement
as Florence crushed Pisa beneath
her spatulate finger-ends again
and the loitering statues made marble remarks.
Only the ranked birds were self-possessed:
the peacock lifted his pea-sized head
and the turkey wattle retained its bronze clots.
The eagle imagined a wind that wasn't there.
In the four corners of the room, meanwhile,
Medici tortoises waved their scaly legs
and, *'festina lente'* wisely said.

IV *Idol*

She with six gold arms,
he with his six: warm,
well-fed, lubricious charm.
His hands hold thunderbolts and prayer bells.
In calm gold faces lax tongues loll.

Her legs encircle him behind
mechanically, like a wind-
up toy wound down, gone blind.
The fat gold god achieves a perfect lotus
but the goddess of celestial coitus doesn't notice.

Atlantic

Their impromptu flung-up chains of wall
only crumble like husk.
How the humpbacked limestone fields mock:
ocean still silts up the cracks of their mouths,
strikes lightning from their flaxen rivers.

Watermark

Among the signs that lovers' bodies give
I loved the slow uncurling of your palms
like beech-leaves making shadows over water:
how my skin was awash for days on end
with the impress of hands on a river.

Marmoreal

Wonder ye then at the fiery hunt?
MOBY DICK

After this warmth the snow must come
to bleach our bodies clean.

It fills our mouths as it falls,
it muffles our cooling bones.

The years collect in drifts about us.
For every ink-stained tryst

there are a thousand blank pages.
And though they'll invoke us like doves

from the howling circle, we'll stare
in silence from our stone address.

Two eyeless statues under snow
blinded by their own bodies' whiteness.

Possession

That anxious way you have of closing doors
(like the brown of your eyes and hair)
was never really yours.
My arms and elongated nose were owned before –
fragments of jigsaw
in the rough art of assemblage whose end we are.

Sometimes I don't know where we live
or whose voice I still
hear and remember
inside my head at night. In darkness and in love
we are dismembered,
so that the fact of our coming to at all

becomes a morning miracle. Let's number
our fingers and toes again.
Do I love you piecemeal
when I see in your closing hand a valve-flower
like a sea-anemone,
or is it our future I remember, as the White Queen

remembered her pinpricked finger? All of you
that's to be known
resides in that small gesture.
And though our days consist of letting go –
since neither one can own
the other – what still deepens pulls us back together.

Lions and Tigers and Bears

Friesians hold the bones of the hills
    inside their tie-dyed pelt. They're
      monochrome mountains draped
        in muddy felt.

The orcas graze and look like them,
    under oceans on the wing.
      The cheetah's greasepaint tears
        absorb the glare

of light from blank savannah eyes.
    Splashed with paw-prints of black ink
      or with a river's ripple
        as the tiger is,

big cats stalk. And your points,
    and mine – that small cinquefoil mole
      like Imogen's under my breast –
        how we wish them

effaced! Distinguishing marks are dangerous
    these days. I lie still, watching across
      your plain white chest the lions,
        the tigers, advance.

A Brief History of Light

And the light shineth in darkness;
and the darkness comprehended it not.

The dazzle of ocean was their first infatuation,
its starry net, and the fish that mirrored it.
They knew enough to know it was not theirs.
Over the hill a dozen furnaces glowed,
the gold gleamed that was smelted in secret,
and the trapped white light shone bitterly
at the heart of the hardest stone on earth.
But they knew enough to know it was not theirs.
Then their hoards of light grew minor,
since none could view the sun straightly,
and jealousy burned their lives to the core.
So they made a god of it, shedding glory,
shedding his light on all their arguments.
Did they know enough to know it was not theirs?
The god in his wisdom preceded them westwards,
and the forests, in whose pillared interiors
black shapes dwelled, were banished for good.
They promised an end to the primitive darkness:
soon there was nothing that was not known.
They thought: *Our light is made, not merely reflected –*
even the forked lightning we have braided!
And they banished the god from the light of their minds.
But they mistook the light for their knowledge of the light,
till light, and only light, was everywhere.
And they vanished in this, their last illumination,
Knowing barely enough to know it was not theirs.

Cedar of Lebanon

The original metaphor
has become the last

that had a deltic beginning
that was fragrant
leaf-lipped and vermilion

casts its shadow momently
on the floor of the pit

Octopus

Mariners call them devil fish,
noting the eerie symmetry
of those nervy serpentine arms.
They resemble nothing so much
as a man's cowled head and shoulders.
Mostly they are sessile, and shy
as monsters, waiting in rock-clefts
or coral for a swimming meal.

They have long since abandoned their
skulls to the depths, and go naked
in this soft element, made of
a brain-sac and elephant eye.
The tenderness of their huge heads
makes them tremble at the shameful
intimacy of the killing
those ropes of sticky muscle do.

Females festoon their cavern roofs
with garlands of ripening eggs
and stay to tickle them and die.
Their reproductive holocaust
leaves them pallid and empty. Shoals
of shad and krill, like sheet lightning,
and the ravenous angelfish
consume their flesh before they die.

A Lecture Upon the Bat

of the species *Pipistrellus pipistrellus*.
Matchstick-sized, from the stumps of their tails
to the tips of their noses. On reversible toes,
dangling from gables like folded umbrellas.

Some of them live for thirty years
and die dangling. They hang on
like the leaves they pretended to be,
then like dying leaves turn dry.

*Suspicions amongst thoughts are like bats
amongst birds*, Francis Bacon writes,
they fly ever by twilight. But commonsense,
not sixth sense, makes them forage at night.

For the art of bat-pressing is not dead.
Inside numberless books, like tiny black flowers,
lie flattened bats. Even Shakespeare
was a keen bat-fowler, or so it's said.

In medieval beast books
extract of bat was a much-prized
depilator. *Reremice be blind as moles,
and lick powder and suck*

*oil out of lamps, and be most cold
of kind, therefore the blood
of a reremouse, nointed upon the legs,
suffereth not the hair to grow again.*

And how toothsome is fruit-bat soup
when boiled in the pot for an hour!
Small wonder then that the Mandarin
for both 'happiness' and 'bat' is 'fu'.

Bats have had a bad press.
Yet they snaffle bugs by the thousand
and carefully clean their babies' faces.
Their lives are quieter than this

bat lore would have us believe.
Bats overhead on frangible wings,
piping ultrasonic vespers. Bats
utterly wrapped up in themselves.

A Weekend in Bodega Bay

Tippi in a pea-green suit and pin-heels.
That sprawling feline smile she wears
ought to be thrown behind bars.
Crows are massing on the jungle jim.
There is the laughter of billions of birds.

Soon the sky is a limited place
full of cries and unbreathable feathers.
It is the watchful malice of women
that maddens them. Tippi
(in heels and a pea-green suit),

watches mother in her kingdom of ruined beauty.
She is driven indoors by the birds
who will eat the palms of her hands.
They leave an awful silence when they go,
a landscape of recumbent, bitten blondes.

Visiting Sergei and Anna

Our journey started from there:
a cursive sweep of railway round the bay,
the indigo stillness of nights punctuated
by the high hum of passing freight,
noise that carried clearer over water...
Leaving Toruń decked in Hanseatic glory
we crossed and recrossed the bridge,
that iron ribcage on a Vistula
pregnant and brooding in the heat,
breeding eels and mosquito nymphs,
thickening to chemical green and brown
the length of its sludgy edge.

*   *   *

At the station boys on national service
thronged the platform with their girls,
thirstily kissing, mouthing massive
syllables through the moving windows.
We concealed ourselves in a sleeper
where everything – the paper cups
and curtains, even the towels and sheets
was stamped with the legend *WARS*.
Though 'scraped flat by the roller'
of our own fatigue we couldn't sleep,
hearing our homesick neighbour
cough and moan his way through Poland.

*   *   *

Do you remember the stuffy dark
of that train, its sudden shuddering halts,
its gathering to pounce forward again
like an animal, its slow lurch south?
There wasn't enough light to see by.
Our blind bodies rocked in their bunks
till the industrial light of six o'clock
showed us Kraków's maze of rails.

In an underground corridor were men
crammed and angled against walls
retching or sleeping in the moist
stink of vinous piss and transit.

*   *   *

I remembered her yellowish eyes,
though I hadn't seen Anna for fifteen years.
In the tiny flat, her lips twitched nervously.
'Sergei is very suspicious.' I noticed
she no longer chain-smoked. 'I have
an operation Wednesday. They take
something out and throw it away.' Then,
'Our canary believes she is a sparrow.'
How brittle its grass-blade legs looked
as it hopped helplessly from perch
to perch in its cage facing the window.
We nicknamed it Tantalus.

*   *   *

Faltering in the dense heat of the market,
her face a semaphore of distress,
she left us at an altar depicting
Mary's assumption from the parish rich:
the mayor, the merchants and even the Jews
carved in relief on the triptych. In Kazimiersz,
where Sergei read Hebrew off the headstones,
was a poplar of such legendary stature
it stood knee deep in the cloud cover.
'After all the sacrifices of those years!
I tell you, my life's profoundest regret is
voting for Wałesa. Now Anna...'

*   *   *

Whose giant hand rang the cathedral bell?
On a high rock was the fortress Waweł,
with its basilica of dead Jagellionians
in saintly sleep under red marble lids.

The dragon who died of silliness and thirst
(drinking the Vistula till his belly burst)
was a pantomime menace at the cave-mouth,
spitting fire to amaze the children.
Taking a train there was like taking
a train from any other place. We agree
there was no irony in the mimeshow
which marked our departure.

*   *   *

On the way I thought of Anna's sparrow
scattering notes like birdseed from
behind the window. 'In the mountains,
there you feel free.' All that talk
of escape, of vocation and solitude,
seemed unjust and noble, making
his eyes a blue scorch in his pale face,
while his wife grew thin as an icon's finger.
Their vast country unrolled in silence
and for hours there were no houses,
just grass and the ground ploughed open,
tracts of what would have been trees.

The Hotel

That hotel we found ourselves uneasy guests of
was like a country house transplanted to the town.
Was it the time of year? We never saw a soul
in the breakfast room, not even a fork was smeared.

The light cord in the bathroom made a violent sound.
Somebody's sock was under the bed.
Our room was full of mirrors – I tried to touch you
but saw my own hand coming towards me.

Yet all it needed was a closer look. What else
were we to do? Our bodies were bloated,
weighty and coarse. We couldn't move an inch.
Our breaths jellified on the bathroom glass

to streaks that looked like condensation.
Was it? In every drop that came from us
we saw a tiny black dot.
I felt a need to agitate the pane.

We saw the ones with tails begin to dance
but the rest stayed still, like the pupils
in a dead eye. They'd never stir again.
Even the jigging ones had so little life

that when we took our breath away they'd cease.
Was this *our* fault, I asked myself?
We left the mean life thriving where it was,
in corners where the spiders hide their eggs.

The breakfast room was full of greying men
who shushed and wagged their fingers and their heads.
It seemed a tribunal, so we left them there
and found our own way out along the stair.

Burning Pig

There's something distracting in a game of chess.
Which is why (pawn to knight five)
I failed to notice as the game advanced

what manner of fuel we had for firing
along with the shreds of Christmas tree.
You gnawed your lower lip, then chanced

your arm in a risky move.
Meanwhile the fire went down.
On turning to the coal-scuttle I winced,

seeing two halves of a divided pig
lying among the Christmas greens.
'You must burn it with the holly,' you announced,

so I threw one half, then the other
on the fire. The poor pig spat
and hissed while the flames danced.

Soon it was transparent wax
except for a lump of its brow and snout,
but as it burned I saw, or rather sensed

the five small fingers of a child
dissolve. And I turned back to the game.
And we finished what we had commenced.

Anxiety

Something had made a killing.
A few small bones by the wall
were sticky with dark blood
but no parts of wing or skull

survived to tell me what it was.
What was it? By afternoon
the petrol-coloured rain had come
and washed it down the drain.

So I wondered if a bird
had ever been killed in a corner
by a wall, and moved off slow
like those pompous burghers

of Oslo do, in *Anxiety*.
But something had made a killing
and the corner worried me
with everything I had, not noticing,

killed. Like those sickish faces
underneath their stovepipe hats,
a yellow shriek of sky behind them
and beyond. It was like that.

Thunder over the Humber

All night the headache has been growing,
the blood gathering to bang in both temples
and with it unease, as though we sensed
that glowering ochre sky-stain over Humber
before like snakebite the lightning comes
unbearably white and silent (its distance
from thunder just an apostrophe between
the echo's voice, the mirror's face)
and inevitably settles on the house
sending the spiders scuttling to their nerve-centres,
while from outside a terrified slow shrill
seeps from the trees, in spite of darkness and rain,
as I overheat, feeling the bedclothes heavier
and, though rational and unafraid,
think of sheeting mirrors and shrouding knives
and of the dark space under the stairs where
(if I didn't know better) I'd willingly blind
and deafen myself, to avoid being struck deaf and blind.

Daffodils

They bring this hint of something startled in them –
the dreadful earliness of their petals
against dead earth, the extremity of their faces
suggesting a violent start –
dumb skulls opening, overnight, to vehemence.
Their lives are quicker than vision,
their voices evade us. And as
water tightens its surface in vases
and sharpens its glass, slicing their sticks
in half, these funnels clatter on their bent necks,
like bells for the already dead.

After a Death

For a whole week
a large emptiness shrieks
endlessly around the hills, made bleak

and salt-striated
under its unabated
sea-stung blast. On my window the desiccated

caked salt
it leaves behind melts,
shatters like sheet ice, and lets the cold bald

February light in.
It startles the walls. We've been
rocked to our own roots too, it seems.

I examine
the gable end for damage,
breakage, and find there a tiny hairline

crack, a replica
in pebble-dash of the Nile delta,
far away on the varicose, split lip of Africa.

My heart knocks
painfully in its small box
of spectacular solitude, whispering to itself, anoxic.

Jaundice results
from pathological blockage of the bile ducts.
Sclerosis. Silting. Failure of flux.

Those spidery
red veins in the yellow eye
she rolled and rolled at me, until the eye congealed,

ignorant of the sun
towards which I, a tree of veins,
an anorexic plant, still shook and leaned.

Flames and Leaves

Dying wasps stagger wide of the mark
though the last of the fuchsia is clotted with pollen.
So autumn gardens discard their red wings.
This late light would char everything
were it not for the fires we deliberately set
from the hacked shreds of the fuchsia bush.
The thing which I greatly feared is come upon me,
and that which I was afraid of is come unto me.
Does the dark have designs on us?
Night rises in its carbon, its nimbus of charcoal stars.

And you are as large as life in my dream,
walking with visible ease
along a river with your daughter and son.
We picnic in the green light from the trees.
I sit cross-legged in your shadow on the grass
hearing the children's laughter drift upstream.
The painter birds you show me through the hedge
weave banners of down and vetch,
dyed with the blood from their blood-red breasts.
What are you losing now but years
that fall away like leaves?
Your once-blue eyes the colour of stained amber.

A Pastoral Murder

(on seeing Tarkovsky's Solaris*)*

I

He makes a bonfire of her life before he goes
to immolate the image of her face
and stands there stoking, her smile as ever
burning him over and over.
He knows the fire will swallow every trace.
Does lightning ever strike an empty house?

II

His final view of the swaying eelgrass
reminds him of her loose hair in the wind.
The rain clears, changing the river-fumes
back into clouds, and as the roan mare runs
he hears in her hoofbeats that sound
the rain made on the leaves before it passed.

Prayer

(after Aleksandr Blok)

Those who were born in the hollow years
are lost and wander blindly.
We are the offspring of Russia's terrors,
Her victims of helpless memory.

Years that left everything burnt and raw,
do you bring madness or hope?
The days of freedom and those of war
baptised us in a bloody stoup.

We are all dumbfounded: the siren
has stopped our mouths that cried.
Hearts that were enflamed now learn
to measure time in the void.

Let our final hours be shared
by the circling raven:
let those who are more worthy, Lord,
be with you today in heaven!

On a Dropped Feather

Until the feather tapers like an arrow
it's a stem of hollow smoky glass
unsnappable from root to subtle tip.
A grounded starling could survive the loss.
This ferny plumage where the shaft begins
is made of down too delicate for flight,
unlike the finny structure of the outer wing,
fashioned for soaring. Perhaps the taut
intrinsic music of a bird comes
from the staves on its small fledged limbs.
The feather's utmost fibres have all the colour
and congruence of shot silk. From the loud strife
and beating of wings in the sky somewhere
it fell like the notched blade of a knife.

Seagulls and Ravens

I

Air thickens in the streets, the lungs.
From sagging cloud-bellies the ravens come
to stalk the park like laryngitic pensioners.

In an effort to calm me, you lick the salt
from my skin. My fingertips have grown eyes.
There is an art to seeing in the dark.

At 3 a.m. a door bangs. I wake calling.
And tomorrow will be heavier, the glass says.
The birds are watching us. They sense our torpor.

II

They are walking out of the night
like giants, out of the dawn.
Their eyes are unkillable embers

over their chests' ashen gourds.
We have effaced ourselves again,
and are nowhere

except in the body's grief.
It falls, what once lay in me.
I turn the colour of ash repeatedly.

Hide

Because it tells me most when it is most alone,
I hold myself at bay to watch the world
regain its level-headedness, as harbours do
when keels are lifted out of them in autumn.
This is not unconsciousness. Seen from above,
the trees are guanoed sea-stacks in a greeny cove
full of gulls' primeval shrieks and waves' extinctions.
Here birds safely crawl between the bushes,
wearing their wings like macs with fretted hems.
The air's a room they fill to bursting with their songs.
All day the common warblers wing it up
and down the scale, see-saw, hammer-and-tongs.
This is not aimlessness. It is something industrial.
A starling cocks its head at a blackbird's coppery top notes.
All I hear of them in the hide reminds me
that the body must displace itself for music,
as my body has, inside this six-inch slot of light.
What converges in a thrush's throat, burnished, tarnished?
Its news endures no longer than the day does.

Thinking of Simone Weil

By day it lives on the other side of the river
in the metallic light that shines through bridges,
light piercing its solitude. Later, its wing-rustle

is the sound night makes over brackish tidal water.
The crane watches, holding a granite pebble
in its featherless claw, as Giraldus tells it,

wakened by the fall of stone into water.
But if the stone escapes the bird's marbled eye
and its iron-digesting throat,

it can do nothing but roll on the floor of the river
to the mountainous blue of the sea-mouth.
Then the sea's concussive weight,

its vast disturbances of pressure, mill the stone
to quartz and its constituents: flint, chalcedony,
amethyst and agate; or again the parts of feldspar:

calcium, potassium, sodium, barium;
and light will flicker through the million minerals
speckling the waves on a deserted beach.

The Nowhere Birds

*In past centuries it was believed that
migrating birds would winter on the moon*

There is no leaving for them
in such shifts south,

best weather is their territory,
their existence its insects

swallowed like distance.
For us, just a surging

of sky-piercing shapes,
pointed birds in search of moon-food,

and the weighty northern day
bereft. But from these beliefs

and from their visiting wings'
return were angels made.

Augury

Magnetic winds from the sun pour in
and send our instruments akimbo.
Nothing runs like clockwork now.
As skeletal clouds unwreathe our exposure,
panicky citizens climb ladders to hammer
their roofs on harder. A crackle of static,
and the world's fat face is in shadow.
There are swallow nests under the eaves,
each with a staring cargo: six bronze bibs,
six black-masked, African birds. They dip
and snap the last bees up. A million Ms
foregather with a million others on the sky.
This is the shape that memory takes.
For days they practise flying, then they fly.